Cold Breath of Life

Cold Breath of Life
a poetry collection

Alyssa Cooper

First Edition

Hidden Brook Press
www.HiddenBrookPress.com
writers@HiddenBrookPress.com

Copyright © 2013 Hidden Brook Press
Copyright © 2013 Alyssa Cooper

All rights for poems revert to the author. All rights for book, layout and design remain with Hidden Brook Press. No part of this book may be reproduced except by a reviewer who may quote brief passages in a review. The use of any part of this publication reproduced, transmitted in any form or by any means, electronic, mechanical, photocopied, recorded or otherwise stored in a retrieval system without prior written consent of the publisher is an infringement of the copyright law.

Cold Breath of Life: A Poetry Collection.
by Alyssa Cooper

Editor – Bruce Kauffman
Cover Design – Richard M. Grove
Layout and Design – Richard M. Grove

Typeset in Garamond
Printed and bound in USA

ISBN - 978-1-927725-02-3

Library and Archives Canada Cataloguing in Publication

Cooper, Alyssa, 1990-, author
    Cold breath of life : a poetry collection / Alyssa Cooper.

ISBN 978-1-927725-02-3 (pbk.)

    I. Title.

PS8605.O653C65 2013   C811'.6   C2013-904146-X

For all the souls
who've broken my heart
in such beautiful ways.

Contents

Forword from the Editor – p xi
Preface – p. xiii

The Stillness of Air – p. 1
Ghost in the Library – p. 2
Blood Letting – p. 3
Crown II – p. 4
Fentanyl – p. 6
Scars on her arms – p. 7
Starry Skies – p. 8
Invisible Horizons – p. 9
Dream Love – p. 10
Just a Nosebleed – p. 12
Kitty – p. 14
Literary Monarchs – p. 15
The Virgin – p. 16
The White Room – p. 17
Canned Goods – p. 19
Rodents – p. 20
Crown – p. 21
Insistent Braying – p. 24
Demolition King – p. 25
Little Birds – p. 26
Crown III – p. 27
Too Close – p. 28
Come back to me – p. 29
Autumn – p. 30
Breakup letter to the sea – p. 31
Chrysalis – p. 33
Fireflies – p. 34
You're a period. – p. 35
He says – p. 36
Splitting Skin – p. 37
Empty Shelves – p. 38
As pure as blank paper – p. 39
Broken Vessels – p. 42
Diviner's Sage – p. 43
Open Windows – p. 44

Tattooed Bones – *p. 45*
Too many teeth – *p. 46*
Numb – *p. 48*
Sickness – *p. 49*
The Exquisiteness of Pain – *p. 50*
Tight Skin – *p. 51*
Tissue Damage – *p. 52*
Thunderclouds – *p. 53*
Stardust – *p. 54*
Spring – *p. 55*
Gravity and Inertia – *p. 56*
He's beautiful like a sapling – *p. 57*
Puzzle Pieces – *p. 58*
Rabbits – *p. 59*
Post Traumatic Stress – *p. 60*
Story of her body – *p. 61*
Mother and Destroyer – *p. 63*
Calm – *p. 64*
Clean Teeth – *p. 65*
He speaks my language – *p. 66*
Moon – *p. 68*
Knotted Muscles – *p. 69*
The Universe – *p. 70*
The Dance – *p. 71*
Distance – *p. 73*
Watching summer die – *p. 74*
Vibration and Sound – *p. 75*
High Tide – *p. 76*
Indian Summer – *p. 77*
Lovesongs – *p. 78*
The Moments After – *p. 79*
Soulmates – *p. 81*
Wings in the sheets – *p. 82*
Poets – *p. 83*
Stay with me – *p. 84*
Satellites – *p. 85*

Acknowledgemants – *p. 87*

Forword from the Editor

In this, her first full collection, Alyssa Cooper proved to me that she is a natural poet, a borne poet. It seems as if these poems flowed to her, through her eyes, her ears, her heart and then flooded out through ink onto the page. I can only imagine the surrender, the joy, and the softness that surrounded her as these poems arrived in the voices of the night—flowing through her as she listened in those moments of silence, epiphany, wonder and tears. This first collection of poetry by Alyssa Cooper is remarkably "brilliant".

    As I approached this manuscript as editor, I became immediately immersed in its depth—not only in a breadth of image and language in the printed lines themselves, but in those innermost spaces between—between the lines, between the words and then between the pages. As I read, in anticipation, turning each page, the next title drawing me in and then each poem after again—washing through. Cascading down, but not like a pouring rain floods the branches and leaves on a tree, but instead gentle like a morning dew falling lightly upon it—each droplet noticed, felt, absorbed, cherished.

    You, the reader, will find in this book poetry that reaches out and touches, and then embraces. These segments of time in time, time in place, time in life—and as the title suggests, the breath flowing within and between. You will sense as well the "cold" in that breath is indeed not a statement of its apathy, but instead its subtle and passive generosity.

    These poems of acknowledgement, of acceptance, and of recognition and of release place themselves here in a flowing sequence. These not like an ocean that lay before us, distant and on its surface—shallow. But instead, much like a wandering stream flowing apprehensively down slow turning bends—inviting us to follow, to explore, to reflect, and to inhale the depth of the beauty of its flow and in all that surrounds. This journey lays itself out throughout this entire collection of poetry and, in particular, her placement of and revisits through the "Crown" trilogy –tearfully heartrending.

    Rumi once said "Sell your cleverness, and buy bewilderment". In this collection of poems, Alyssa Cooper has done that—and given it back.

Bruce Kauffman, Editor

Preface

Cold Breath of Life is the diary of a strange and twisted five year journey, cataloguing each stop along the way. From my first heart rending tragedy, Just a Nosebleed, to my youngest elegy of hope, Soulmates, this collection weaves together all the confusion and ecstasy that came along with my metamorphosis from past to present. It is a carefully constructed portrait of everything that has fallen behind me.

There was a time when my words were constructed, when every sentence showed effort and strain, and not a touch of passion. But the new millennia was an era of great change for me. It took time for me to know myself, but when I did, the first of the poems that laid the foundation for this collection were written. They surprised even me with their honesty.

At first I was embarrassed to have laid myself so naked on the page, but a moment later, I knew better. I knew that there was nothing to be ashamed of; I was proud. I would never give in to expectation again. I had found the beauty of truth.

The road was slow at first, with stops and halts and moments of self doubt, but soon the ink flowed like a river from my pen. My voice refused to be silenced.

Sometimes, the words that live your head and sleep on your tongue just have to come out. It doesn't matter the form or the style; those words are pure feeling, and they are desperate to be unleashed. Sometimes it feels like I'm an afterthought, just the one who organizes the chaos of language; a curator to the exhibition of my own tangled emotions. But I'd demand nothing more. I am grateful for these words.

Whether harshly literal or deeply metaphorical, the poems in this collection explore the many facets of the human experience. Love and loss, joy and despair, mania, depression, and lucid calm; in these last five years, I've felt them all. I've lost friends in countless numbers, and I've found love in a wasteland. I've seen my mother step to the edge of death, and I've seen the strength of my family pull her back, while others around us were not so lucky. I've let the world break my heart and stitch me back together at the fault lines; I have lived. And somehow, in the aftermath of all these things, I was able to find the words for every moment. And that's what waits between these pages. Open your mouth, close your eyes, and ready for your lungs for the cold breath of life.

Alyssa Cooper

The Stillness of Air

The alluring and intolerable stillness
of air,
winter hanging on spring,
desolate landscapes where winds stop short,
and sound
falls silent.

A seeming bend in time and space,
a pause;
the molecules stop moving.
My breath,
it stops
   within my lungs.

Fall to the earth,
with tree root fingers grasping,
a buck skull in my belly.
Soak in the stillness;
   that moment like death,
until the world
comes back
   to life.

And when it does,
in that instant,
   I am lost.

Ghost in the Library

I am a creature
of oblivion.
I feast on air, and memories,
    and scraps of poetry.
A ghost in the libraries,
my soul escapes to sing over fields
    as I sleep.

I wander haunted moors
    with my black Irish eyes,
under a sky of thick
dark paint.
A creature of constant motion,
refusal of rest,
    I burn my flesh like fuel;
    I am distributed into
the universe.

I will reduce myself
to the essential,
    nothing but bones;
grind them up to blow away
the dust,
    and then I can finally prove
you don't need wings to fly.

Blood Letting

Summer comes again,
with hot days
and nights that refuse
    to end.
The perfect time
to clean my veins.

Ancient princes
with dripping wrists,
a princess draped in gold
    and dangling rubies;
the scarificator
with clicking teeth like a music box;
that singing pain
    to calm
my shaking hands.

Crown II

She makes me think of someone wonderful,
       but I can't place her.
Someone
with spun sugar lips
and short fur hair,
       spots like a jaguar,
and thin, lithe
       muscles
run through with tendons;
she's a feline.

Maybe I never
       knew her.
Maybe I dreamt her;
I swear I made her up.
Her body,
her photographs,
       her life.
That unrelenting sadness.

She lives disconnected,
an inch
       above the ground.
Too beautiful,
she has wings,
that we can't see.

Tethers, weights; her ties
       a curse.
The unbearable burden of solidity;
The weight of her flesh.
She belongs to heaven,
       and there's only one escape.

I learn acceptance
       from a ghost,
discover beauty
in the sweetest words
of all:

       "Nothing will last
          forever."

Fentanyl

Her painkillers delivered through patches,
stuck one day on her arm
    the next on her back,
    the next shoulder,
    then hip,
and they leave behind
    rashes.
They turn red
and itch.

She tells them all,
  "My bones hurt,"
and really she means
  "Without them,
    I ache
      down to my bones."

This is, of course,
a subtle difference.

Scars on her arms

She has scars
on her arms.

I saw them
when she meditated.

I'd never ask,
never deign to voice those questions.
But knowing,
it comforts me.

It soothes.

Starry Skies

The sky will be
           white
before the world dies.

Invisible Horizons

The clouds broil up to meet me,
thick swaths
of blue
   and yellow,
like paint from the jar,
pushed along
by my invisible brushes.

I can lift off
   the pavement,
weightless and floating,
as if my body were
left behind.
I could fly away.
Just a little more time,
a little more
   strength,
and I could make it.

Past the rooftops,
so many black pyramids
in the dusky, dreamtime
   glow,
past the right-angled bloodlines
that fall to waste
below my feet,
past all that hard edged structure
and to the forest,
that soft smudge of freedom
that blurs
   my horizon.

Dream Love

On the darkest nights,
when her sleep won't come easy,
she crawls into my bed
    and drowses,
and her dreams leak through her skull.

I would never
    dare
to touch her.
She's just so beautiful sleeping.

There's nothing between us,
nothing there
that she would share in feeling.

For me,
she is love
    and terror,
and a careful amalgamation
    of heat
    and breath
    and lust and restraint.
And resentment…
And adoration…

Hers is blood
that has stood the test
    of time.
I've never seen it flow,
but I know
that she has.

In my dreams,
her scars are thin
    red
    lines.

My regret solidifies;
causes the stomach
to ache.
    Butterflies burst out of my skin
    and they carry my heart on tenuous,
        luminous
fibres.

I could not tell you her name.

Just a Nosebleed

I lay beside him,
and he slept.
  Our first night together,
    sacred.
And with him,
I found a truth,
burning;
I saw his face, peaceful in sleep,
    beautiful.
I remembered his eyes,
perfection.

But there was something
    else,
something different,
and the realization was
    horrible,
but painless.
Like a wound cut so deep,
  it doesn't even hurt anymore.
Dark blood, hot tears,
  but no pain.

  And I realized how I loved him,
  but I knew the truth,
    knew he'd never say the same.

And I had to let go.

Like a wound cut so deep,
it doesn't even hurt anymore.
Like a nosebleed;
dark blood,
but no pain.

Our love was something beautiful;
    tragic.
But my loss –

just a nosebleed.

Kitty

My cat brings me
dead mice,
leaves them at my door
with bloody fur,
      broken bones.
And I praise him,
and pet
      until he purrs
        his satisfaction.

He kills birds,
piles the tiny bodies on my
      porch.
Various states of decay,
with cloudy eyes lolling
      toward empty sockets.

I move the corpses
      with a shovel,
and I praise kitty.
I pet
his murderous head.

Literary Monarchs

My failures ring truer
than any success,
a queen of broken hearts
and swollen eyes;
never a princess,
but a monarch,
ruling head of literary tragedies,
 of irony
and symbols,
taking the place of any brand
 of happy ending.

This is my kingdom,
Plath and Eugenides,
my predecessors.
The crown,
it doesn't quite
 fit,
but I'll fill it someday.
I grow
with every heartbreak.

The Virgin

She sits
on the banks of a river,
a young girl,
a white dress,
with a notebook open
      on her knees
as hundreds of tiny snakes
twist
in the mud at her feet;
twist,
and writhe.

And she writes:
      Sometimes the words
      come easy,
           others,
      I am squeezing milk
      from
           a stone.

The White Room

It is an empty room;
>tall white walls
>and pale
>wooden
>floors.

No windows,
>no ceilings.
It goes up and up,
forever,
>up she goes;
>up she goes.

I can lock up
wanton thoughts
in my heavy
>wooden chest.
There is
no key;
>the things that go in,
>they don't need
>to come out.

The ghosts in my mind
>won't hush,
hushaby hushaby,
and their words
>pour forth
with frightening intensity,
intensity in whispers,
>so hard to understand;

    stop talking over
                      each other,
    stop talking over
                      each other,
    STOP TALKING OVER
                      EACH OTHER.

But there is no door
    to my white room.
No windows;
seamless.
They cannot enter,
and I,
I fear the moment
    of my own escape.

Canned Goods

Hair falling into the sink,
swirling down the drain;
but then it returns,
      twisted,
crawling back up
to take over
      my body.

Bleeding gums
and streaming nose,
I eat like a hobo,
      straight from the can,
the juices dripping down my chin.

It's been
      days,
and I am

      alone.

Rodents

Black bead eyes,
    all cold
    and blank
    and empty,
glittering in the sunshine,
staring,
staring with nothing inside.
I'd set my traps
    if I could,
I'd collect them.
I'd use buckets of water,
    and long
    thin
    knives.
I'd make sure those eyes
wouldn't ever look
    that way
again.

Crown

The day I heard the news,
    it came not through meeting
    or even phone call,
but from the cold eyes
and careful distance
of a well-structured article, written by a man
    who lived a half a world away.

I felt the loss not in my heart
but in my stomach,
with a tightness that seemed
    inappropriate
to the length and meaning
of our infrequent conversations.

Later,
I found the meaning of her name.
Now,
when I speak of her,
that meaning plays like a chant
in the deepest part
    of my skull.

I thought there must be something,
some symbolism
my writer's mind could cling to.
But it's been four years now,
    a solid length of contemplation,
    and still,
I've found nothing.

"Sweet tooth burns a hole in your head —"
Rainbow suckers,
caught on her sugary lips;
    there is more for me in that
    than in crowns.

Of course I saw no funeral.
That same faraway journalist
    allowed me photos,
but the high res images
of the
    long
    black
    car
were like pornography.
    My stomach again,
    and not my heart,
felt the pain and shame in equal measures,
and so I looked
    no further.

And now my crown lies melting,
under the grass,
in a place that I know I will probably never see.
When the loss was new,
I sculpted a marble marker,
    a lonely plot in my mind,
and I kneeled before it to speak to her,
nothing to offer
    save lamentation.

But now,
I find that I am ready to offer honour
    to her life,
and pay respect to more
    than just the points at either end
        of that line.

The words from this pen tonight
are hers,
    from me;
a solemn word weaver she barely knew.
A stranger
who still remembers her bones.

Insistent Braying

There's a dog at the gate,
barking,
braying and spitting,
with red eyes
and mange.
He paces,
on bleeding paws
with tapping nails,
a stutter step,
a dance,
thin legs with heavy cords
and gouging, leaping ribs.
His breath comes hard,
with gasp and spray,
until his eyes
roll.
But he won't fall silent.
His braying
insists.

Demolition King

It feels like I'm exploding,
    like I'm fading;
how can I feel both
at once?
I'm sleeping beauty,
the demolition king –
    wait,
was that a touch
    too contradictory?
It feels like waking up,
it feels like dying.
    Certainly,
that can't be true.

Snow in summer,
under ice in
    July.
Freezing to death
in an inferno.
Being born,
    or
massive organ failure.

I don't even know
who I am.

Little Birds

I watched hawks feast
    on little birds,
snapping beaks
and flashes of blood;
they tore the meat up
in strips,
and bright feathers
    fluttered,
        colourful.
Tiny bodies,
hollowed out
    before me.

Crown III

Once a year I burn
    your photos
celebrating your birth;
remembering
your slender face,
your body,
made up of hills and valleys,
    curves and slopes,
dusted in shadow.

You were so beautiful,
    once,
a painted virgin queen,
with marble skin
and dark doe eyes,
and I'm sure you felt
    beautiful,
then,
in that last moment,
as you threaded
    the noose.

I'm sure
    you tried,
dressed for a party and
swinging
in the sunshine.
But no one leaves
    a beautiful corpse;
there is no beauty

in death.

Too Close

When I say her name
my heart stops beating,
and without her,
I cannot breathe.
I blur the fine line
between love and obsession –
not an overabundance
    of love,
but a lack of it;
I study her like fossils,
with fascination.
I observe and treasure,
and maybe,
this isn't love. Maybe,
I've come too close.

Come back to me

It's been so long alone,
so many years of winter
      without you.
So many seasons have passed,
long days in the cold, dark, blue;
      in the silver wrap of silence.

I ache to see you
      bathed in light,
the way that you were
when you left.
Do you think of me where you are,
in the haze of your overestimated confusion?
Do you remember endless summers
      in sepia tones?

I yearn for you.

It's so hard
to find the words,
to force my thoughts into something
      so trivial.
Impossible to find my voice,
when my body,
      my shaking, shivering, aching
      body,
knows exactly what it is
that I need to say;

'I miss you,
I love you.
Come back to me.

Come home.'

Autumn

In fall we watch the wind.
The grass under our feet
starts to freeze,
and we will throw leaves
      in handfuls.
Handfuls of fire,
as our hot fingertips
turn to ice.

In fall we drink ciders,
sharing sloppy kisses
with wet
      sweet
         mouths.
We roll in leaves,
down hills,
until we are wet
and musty like the earth.

We run with pink cheeks,
      red noses,
the fire of autumn caught up
in my hair.
Our feet pound glistening frost,
and we will find that speed
      doesn't matter.
We could never outrun
the winter.

Breakup letter to the sea

The widow's peak,
stretching up over cliffs,
reaching out
   across the waves.
I watch the churning sea,
that broiling pot
  of blue and green,
bubbling streaks of white
and hidden shadows
  of purple,
    indigo;
all those royal shades,
calling from the undertow.

Did I make the most
of loving you?

Salted air,
wet,
wet and heavy,
cleaning out my lungs,
beading
in my hair.
Deafened by the crash,
the roar of the water
so far below.
Seductive waves,
   cold,
    waves that clamber
and bash,
climbing the cliffs
with consciousness;

reaching out for me.
tugging me
  to the edge.

The peak is my post...
But how can I write of seas
that I have never seen?

Chrysalis

Somewhere
between a dream and a miracle;
    but possible, still.
Tiny purple veins,
delicate like spiders' silk,
painted across her skin.

Pressed together,
until the air turned to steam,
    and oxygen
    was gone;
until everything
blurred.

Wet lashes
    and dry lips;
salt clogs up every orifice,
so that I can't see,
    or speak,
    or breathe.
I could collect them,
I swear,
and bathe in those waters,
and come out the other side
    something else.

Fireflies

Once upon a different world,
we glowed like coals,

burning embers on the hearth.

We shone and gleamed,
fireflies

    in a jar,
    without a single hole
    in the lid.

You're a period.

A cemetery
in the forest,
a twelve pronged buck
standing over my grave.
This is you,
the memory of you,
a phantom
      in my mind.

It offsets my teeth;
      they click,
and the pain
      is sharp,
little broken bones,
shards,
      in my mouth.

I don't think of you,
not anymore,

and you,
      you can't make me
      sweat.

I finally
      gave up on you.

Don't ever come back.

He says

"I should tell you
how this feels,"
    he says,
"You're a writer,"
    he says,
"You can use it.
It's in my back
and inside my chest,"
    he says,
"Like a family
dying,"
    he says.

And I pray for silence.

Splitting Skin

As I sheared my hair
away from
    my scalp,
it seemed a symbolic gesture.

Not teenage rebellion,
no coming
    of age;
much more meaningful
than that.

A shedding of old things,
arching my back to split
    my skin,
split it wide,
so that I felt for the first time
the cold breath of life
on my clean
    new
        flesh.

Empty Shelves

A mind like a bookstore,
sectioned off,
all neat and clean.
Forgotten volumes hiding,
tucked away
on the wrong shelves,
texts hidden
in foreign lands.
A cluttered back room
without light
and locked doors,
stuffed to bursting with all the books
that never made
    the shelves.

As pure as blank paper

I've been locked inside for
I don't know how long;
    I've lost time.
Barred the doors,
    boarded up the windows,
denying disturbance.

I no longer
    know dawn.
I'm awake and it could be
    night,
    could be day,
it could be
    another world,
and none of that matters.

At first I had the typewriter,
with its tapping metal keys,
    every word, every line
    a violent beating;
until that black river of ink
ran dry,
betrayed me,
but it was still no excuse
    to stop.

These words hold passion,
a history of something
    I cannot name.
They sleep within my blood,
waking;
seeping through my open pores.
    I cannot let them be lost.

There is no excuse to stop.
   This,
my only need.

So now those pages
with their neat, clean lines,
are somewhere under the pages
of erratic pen strokes
that followed;
   my own unique blend
   of cursive and print.

The vehicle of these words is
barely relevant.
   Barely. Barely,
   if at all.

I burn the furniture for heat,
tearing apart
   the frames,
blood and soot on my fingers
that I must wash away;
I can't bear to leave stains
on something as pure
   as blank paper.

Between pages I rest
but never sleep;
my dreams flow out through my fingertips,
   no need to close my eyes.
I've lost my yearning for comfort,
my meat reduced
   to machine.

These words are the weightiest
part of me;
    all of these sounds
      make me solid,
and each and every word I weave
    brings me closer.

I'll pour out my presence,
leave my life behind on paper,
a heap that grows,
    and grows,
    and grows,
blue pen strokes concealed now
by wet, dark ink splatters
and tiny, tiny
    brushstrokes.

Growing tall enough to carry me,
to lift me to the rafters.
    By then there'll be nothing left;
    a sheet of blank paper.
I'll float out through the ceiling,
carried on a breeze.

I'll fly away;
I'll leave.
I'll leave my locked-up room of poetry
far, far behind.

Broken Vessels

She cries so much.
Her tears drip
over her body,
      sliding
over her bruises,
all those shades
      of thunderclouds.

The neighbours,
they think that I beat her.
And I let them.

It is easier
than telling them;
they would never
      understand.

Sometimes,
      she wakes up shaking,
      shivering.
Fighting,
so that the only way
to calm her
is to hold on
   so tight
that her vessels

      burst

under my love.

Diviner's Sage

The boy inhales deep,
and at the moment
      of understanding,
laughter bursts.
It shatters his skin,
builds up a path
      to be followed;
a path
that speaks.
He is eaten,
      swallowed,
and is born again
into lightness;
he finds solace
in his ascension.

Open Windows

You're a voice inside my head now.
I've opened every window,
    but you won't leave.
I travel at sea, a whispering breeze,
I'm a current in the ocean
and you're there;
    still there.
I can't get away,
I try to fly on clipped wings,
red ribbons streaming from the scissor cuts,
    but you're stuck in every thought now.
    You are my every thought,
    angelic possession,
    my words my breath my pain oh god
        please stop.

I'm locked inside my head with you.
I've sought solace in sister Sleep,
but I've slept away the months now;
    exhausted, always.
Losing meat,
it melts so that my bones show,
so that I get scared
when I run my fingers down my spine;
bulging hills from hip to neck,
    but I can't bring myself to eat.

I need to expunge you from my brain,
    claw you away,
    but you won't come loose.
I count the seconds as they pass,
    tick tock tick,
        numerology to keep you at bay.

But you slip in with every sweep
 of the clock hand,
an instant between instants,
 a banging in my brain.

I've opened every door,
every window;
 but you won't leave.

Tattooed Bones

A child of the '90's,
born
in the dark,
I am child-sized.
Eternal youth, I'm a vampire;
like Bathory,
I bathe in the blood of virgins.

I appropriate the ages,
stitched together
like a rag doll,
stealing from the dead,
the forgotten;
I'm a gravedigger.

Let every life I steal
leave a mark;
let them peel back
my skin,
and tattoo my bones.

Born a blank mannequin,
white and smooth.
But now,
I have my fangs;
my wings,
   my stripes,
and all great things grow
of humble beginnings.

Too many teeth

She threw herself against him,
such force,
so that the air
    rushed
from his lungs,
even as her lips closed
    over his,
determined to suck away
the last of his
breath.

She has too many
    teeth,
as she moves
with a thousand tongues,
but..
she's beautiful.

Through all the
horror
and tiny shining secrets,
past the
    lies
she holds like candies,
he takes her over,
pushing his way behind the vice
of her undecipherable
    lips.

Through all this silently
    gasping
    passion,
he will learn.
He will come to find that her blood
    tastes like ice.

Numb

Skin and bones,
I've carved away the parts
that don't belong.
I've found
    the control;
steadied my metaphysical
knife,
and found something so close
to perfection.

And I am *happy*.

I have no illusions
    of grandeur;
I know that I'm dying,
but these days,
    it's painless.
I'm numb.

Beautiful,

and sweetly
        numb.

Sickness

So sick,
a swelling inside my veins,
so that blood
can't pass;
no lymph or melancholy;
everything
stands still.
We've approached the speed of light,
the clocks have fallen silent;
and my chest, too,
its pulse has stopped,
the blood clotting
within the still caverns
of my many chambered heart.

The Exquisiteness of Pain

Cloaked figures chant,
swinging censors in callous hands.
The shadows leap,
   leap and sing,
and on the altar,
I sing along.
Lips break open;
   bleed,
dripping red on my serpents' tongue.

I am not real,
   here.
I am a sinning shade,
come to worship.
Violated virgin,
the madonna swollen
   with hope.

I will give birth
to my saviour.

The shadows chant,
a steady defiance of dead eyes,
but with my hands on my skeleton,
   I remember you.
They have never known you
in the ways that
I have known you.
They will never know
the exquisiteness of pain.

I
am the lucky one.

Tight Skin

There are tree roots just under the surface,
pressing blue
against my white skin.
They spread and branch,
gasping for life,
suffocating on the inside,
my skin too tight;
    too thick;
    too heavy;
I can't bear this weight,
the close, closing pressure
of physicality.
I can't stand
to be real.

Tissue Damage

A harsh rush
of venomous hate;
this is something I've never felt
before.
A shock of heat that snaps
over and over,
leaving welts,
welts that swell across my back
and chest,
that leave scars. I'm not sure;
will they ever heal?

A mass of worms,
squirming in my stomach,
in the emptiness I call a chest,
cold little worms,
frozen,
blocks of ice.
They would spread through my veins,
if they could only find the path.
And they will poison everything
as soon as they break through.

Thunderclouds

Bruises
just under the skin.
Not quite purple,
but dark,
   a stain,
tiny like thumbprints,
scattered;
unplaceable.
They bloom and ache,
their presence
   insistent,
but they die quiet.
They fade away
without a word,
so that the lack of pain
   is a shock.
A surprise,
that causes you to press
and poke,
to pester for the memory
of the ache that used to live there.

Stardust

Everything is branching,
   reaching…
Limbs and veins and
roots.

Reassembled from star dust,
I am nothing
that I said I would be.

Spring

The sun came out this morning,
fell through barren branches
and painted my white winter skin
with shimmering gold
and broken shadow joints.

The warmth cut through the wind,
the fire of sunlight
burning up the icy chill,
the rushing screaming air
chasing away
winter demons.

Light lit up the shadows,
giggling, babbling, gurgling rays
banishing the darkness;
laughter chasing off the grey.

The world growing back into youth.

Gravity and Inertia

Who was it that said
my arms
are not built for flight?
Who was the one
that clipped my wings?

Newton,
who tied my feet to the earth,
Mister Kepler
and his inertia;
I owe
    no tithe
to the men who hold me,
    so tight and still,
against the earth.
I'll pay homage instead
to the one
    who has lifted me
so high.

I'll bend my arms
like wings,
and let them carry me
    away;
I'll move through the sky
like water,
like Icarus,
skimming my fingertips across
    the sun,
without the fear
of falling.

He's beautiful like a sapling

The seeds I planted
were weak,
the soil never tilled;
I could have sworn
that the earth they laid in
    was toxic.
But in the face of drought,
the stalks
pushed up
    to the sun.
They turned their faces to glory,
and they bloomed;
they became
    beautiful,
in spite of
my poorly tended garden.

Puzzle Pieces

I fell in love
before I had the words.
The feelings came alone
independent of language;
until I pieced together all the facets
of our adoration,
and found the shape of the puzzle
new,
yet still
    oddly
    familiar.

I was just in time for him,
that boy who didn't sleep with me
that night,
even though
    he could have,
the one who's taken over
my every
thought,
swallowing down
my waking moments
and chewing through
my sleep,
so that I'd rather
watch him in the moonlight
than close my eyes and give in
    to rest.

So that suddenly,
I'm one of those
assholes
who believes that every moment
    is precious.

Rabbits

When I leap
from my window,
I seem to glide
    for miles,
moving in slow motion,
lighter
than air.

I always hit the ground
    running,
pushing harder,
changing
to allow the movement;
the freedom.

Running like the rabbits
leaping
    across my scars;
the rabbits that lead me
    to sunset.

Post Traumatic Stress

As a woman she will wake in the night,
flustered and disturbed,
and she will barely remember.

Story of her body

There is a stranger
at my window,
but I barely see him
    through curtains.

There's a woman on one side of me,
    a man on the other,
holding my hands as we lie together,
in the dark.
She whispers,
"He's here
for you."
And he whispers,
"He's here
    for the story."

But the shape behind the glass
    has vanished.
The curtains flutter
around an empty space.

Together they murmur
"Let me show you,"
and sit me up
and stretch out my arms
so that I can see the words
wrapping up and up
    in tiny black letters.

Their fingertips run across my back,
and in overlapping voices,
they tell me my tale.

Lost on the rise and fall,
    the hum of their words,
I start new lines
    on the marble
of my thighs.

One in each ear,
they tell the tale of my past,
while in unreadable symbols,
    I lay down the next chapter.

Mother and Destroyer

I am an observer;
I watch
and listen,
but do not speak.

There's a cheshire cat smile
in the sky tonight.
Barely a sliver,
    a hook,
a hook with sharp ends
to reach under my flesh.
A full and glowing orb
would hold no power,
but that crescent of light
calls up an all new breed
    of lycanthrope.

I run through the night,
like a cheetah,
a study in speed
and long, thin muscles.
My anatomy changes;
    accommodates
this foreign flow.

The night,
It bleeds like ink,
and me, I turn
    rabid;
I howl
and scream,
a wild dog
with festering wounds.

Two sides of the coin;
I am mother,
    and I am destroyer.

Calm

The quality of my introspection
may not match
    my elders,
but it is
powerful.
I know words
that even they have never heard
    before;
I have felt the things
they have dreamed
of feeling,
but never
    achieved.

I am still
in my resolution.
In the face of
    loss,
I have found
    only gain,
and for the first time
that I can remember,
    I am calm.

Clean Teeth

His teeth clamping down
on my joints,
my dainty wrists
and coltish knees,
as if he'll swallow them
    down
all at once,

the sounds of rushing air
and swelling heat;
his pulse
    just under the surface,
the sounds
of his anatomy
as we move through
    our dream,
occupying
the same small space.

Overlapping.

I can feel the mark he leaves
    on my skin,
a burn that lasts long after
he's gone.
Constant reminders;
his hard, straight
    teeth
and soft, insistent
hands.
I can find the trails he's walked
with my blind eyes.
No need for
    sight,
in the face of his

inferno.

He speaks my language

Writing poetry
    for love;
it's never been
my style,
but oh,
the things you've done
    to me.

You make me feel like a flood
    of words,
in the perfect order;
you touch me like
    a sonnet.
You are the twists of English language
that I've spent a lifetime
    aching
to discover.
You are the beautiful and mythical
spellings
of Gaelic,
so lost to me
    still,
and yet
so dear,
    so close.

You are the words that
    drip
from between my lips,
and hang like beads
on a glistening
    string.
You are finger-tip messages
left in breath
on my
    windows,
you are the thumbnails
of poetry,
scrawled across

    my skin.

Moon

The experience of being
        one,
of opening
into a billion glowing particles
and floating
        through the world.

Constant flow,
a fading ebb.
        I can feel the tides,
        pulled,
by the broad white face
of the glowing
        moon.

Knotted Muscles

The hands on the clock
keep turning,
marking every second
that keeps us
apart.
Days fade,
and hours
    spread;
I breathe you in,
deeper,
    deeper,
        deeper.

My heart is
    beating
in your hands,
a hard little
knot
of tension,
and I'll follow you
forever –

how could I not?

How could I live
    without my heart?

The Universe

You are a universe; such gravity!
I will break apart on your surface,
I will lose control in this heat,
I will leak into your tightened veins.
My hollow bones will
    shatter
within your beating heart.

You are a gasp of air in this alien world.

I am drowning in your eyes,
I am burning against your skin,
you're breaking me, bruising me;
    beautiful blood leaking under my skin.
    My aching pulse.

I'm lost in your mouth,
a heat that could thaw the winter,
I'm gasping for your breath.
    Pulling, pushing, needing.

We are Abelard and Heloise,
    Tristan and Ysolde,
we are the greatest of all the lovers.
Ours is a story
told in the spaces between lines;
    told less by what is said
    than what is not.

I am deafened by your heartbeat,
and I swear I'll never rest
    until I find my way back under your skin.

The Dance

The tracks;
they are aware and alive
tonight,
as we wait together
for the train that will once again
tear us apart.

The colourless concrete
and the fresh emerald grass
clash grotesquely.
But in the West are
billowing, boiling clouds
that pull our scene together.

Leaves and petals cascade
around us,
forming a dream.
In the ink-stained sky,
thunder cracks.

A single raindrop –
like ice –
on my shoulder;
a prelude to the storm.

In frustration and adoration
I throw myself upon him,
my arms around his neck,
and bite,
tasting salt on his hot skin.

From the North,
winds blow hard,
kicking up sand and
stinging pebbles,
until our young flesh is
raw
and burnt.

In the air is the scent
of a garden;
flowers dedicated to dead babies,
to a girl who never
loved
like we do.

And on the zephyr,
we find a rhythm.

We spin and dance
like fools.
At arms length;
tripping - stumbling;
grinning and laughing in the absence
of music.

But on the inside,
we are slow dancing,
and he croons,
because his ride to hell comes
soon.
The seasons are changing
fast.
And God,
who knows when the next dance will be.

Distance

My name is Destiny.
My name is distance.
My shame is separation.

Watching summer die

Today,
the summer betrayed me.
The warmth slunk away
while I slept;
a beaten dog.
It crept
into the shadows,
bringing back cold,
and wind, and despair.
Today,
the sun has died,
and in a haze of desperate,
melancholic
despair,
the funeral plans begin.
Barren lonely fields
and cold, blue light.
This is what the summer leaves behind.

Vibration and Sound

The strumming of guitar strings,
    a ball dropped to play a note.
I am vibration and sound,
empty,
endless.
I am hollow,
    holes cut clean through,
    a violin.

    I keen
    and screech,
my anguished song torn free
by barbed wire bows,
    by skeleton hands,
and all the worst intentions.

My chest is a vacuum.

I'll never be able to forget
    this feeling.

High Tide

We move like waves
beating
against the shore,
turning our face
    to the moon,
and praying
for high tide.

We twist
and turn,
and you invent
    knots
I've never seen before,
a beautiful rope-work
that binds us,
intricate loops
with Celtic names,

until I'm losing track
of where I end and you
    begin;
buried so deeply
    in your skin.

Indian Summer

I could have sworn
this summer would last
    forever;
just weeks ago,
I was sure of it.
Sure of the golden light
that dances on the air,
and sure
of the hot winds
that rip
    through my clothes.

I'll sleep
through separation,
until winter has no more power
    than a dream.

For me, spring comes after
    the summer;
I'll pass by autumn,
and evade the biting
winter,
and my sun will rise
    on new life,
on tiny bodies,
like smiles,
born up out of the
    earth.

Lovesongs

Your teeth behind your lips
play chords for me,
your tongue plucking strings
as the scent of your throat
    sings,
waking me up,
as if it's morning;
as if you are the sun
    rising
beyond my window.

You're the one who brings my words
    to the surface,
and you stitch them together
with your wandering
    hands,
sculpting my poetry
into lyrics;
only you can give me
    my melody.

And these are the days
that I can't bear
    the silence.

The moments after

The scene of our crime
can't match the purity of our union;
in the moments after, I reflect.
    Ragged, peeling wall-paper,
    water stained ceiling, bleeding grey,
    even the curtains, innocent lace, are
    ripped, fraying; yellowed
and dark.
The blankets, tangled in knots around us,
offer a faint smell of mildew;
    of ancientness, dampness,
    still air.

Not long ago,
we were heaving breath
and racing hearts;
    my skin, it flushed to scarlet,
    his sweat dampening my hair.
But this is the winding down time.
    These are the moments after.

Through his fingers, I can catch
his memories.
His hair on my face,
brushing my cheeks,
catching on parted lips and
fluttering
    with my breath.

My heart skipped
at the touch of his hot palms,
    scalding,
        lighting up my skin
with explosions, tiny fires.
His hands trailing over me
are a reminder,
the epilogue to our act
    that makes past feel like prologue.

I can taste the salt of his throat,
drifting on the pull and swell
of his rhythmic breath,
    his beating heart.

I am safe,
safe in the warmth of this stolen night
and this feeling,
    contained inside an impure room.
The total lack of control,
and sense,
and rationality;
    this was only a precursor.

I am most alive here,
    in the moments after.

Soulmates

You'll find me trapped in the sheets
long after
    I'm gone;
I swear, I'll never leave.
I will persist;
I will
    endure.

You speak
    like music;
every story becomes
a song,
a melody lodged inside
my brain,
so I couldn't claw it free
even if
    I wanted to.

I don't believe in soulmates,
    not really;
but you make me wish
that I did.
You make me wish for long days
and never-ending

    summers.

Wings in the sheets

These are the roads
I take home,
lined with
    locked doors,
    and bridges
burned to the ground.

You left your
    heart
in the sheets,
to wrap around me
like wings,
to bind me,
    blind me,
to tie my hands

too tightly.

Your smile rises
like the sun;
the dawn can't come
    without you.
The kind of beauty that
infects,
    and inspires,
a joy that bubbles
in the heat of adoration.

Poets

I have no urge
    for stories
these days.
I'm deep in my role
as writer,
and for consumption like breathing,
I crave
    poetry.

Beautiful poetry,
that inspires me,
inspires me to be
    truthful
and
    vulgar.
To be real.

With plain and pretty
    language,
telling those deep and soulful
    tales,
so that you can hear them,
their voices,
so that they speak to you
with every
    word.

Stay with me

In my mind
I'm still in bed with you,
    languishing
as the sun comes up around us.

I miss you
    desperately
already,
petting my hair
and crooning,
wrapping up around me,
stretching
and pulling
and making fun
    of ticklish feet.

'Stay with me
    tonight,
please,'
words I keep hearing
long after silence
    surrounds;
vigor and chivalry,
and our blood,
flooding our cheeks with every smile
that we could never
    hide.

Satellites

I am a moon trapped in orbit,
a satellite
doomed to spin,
the sweetest brand
of damnation,
my tight little circles,
over and over,
around the burning sun
of your adoration.

Never coming closer,
gravity holds the distance,
holds my heart at bay;
to come too close is suicide,
an agonizing plunge
into the centre of your heat,
an end that I long for.
Not quite irony,
but fitting,
this longing for an end,
a love with an expiration date.
A moon for now,
spinning in my circles,
a satellite;

but we all fall someday,
whether its an abyss that waits,
or paradise.
And me,
I'm ready for the plunge.

I'm ready for the sun.

Acknowledgemants

– "Just a Nosebleed," *Immortal Verses*. Massachusetts: Newton Rhymes, LLC, 2008.

– **"The Moments After,"** *The Poetic Pinup Revue*, August Issue, 2012.

– "The Universe," *The Poetic Pinup Revue*, August Issue, 2012.

– **"**watching summer die," *Revival Literary Journal*, Issue 23, 2012.

– "Autumn." Stone Voices Literary Showcase, *Inspired by Joy*. May 2012. <http://www.stonevoices.co/uploads/files/CooperSUM12.htm>

– The Virgin. 5 Poetry Journal, Issue #9. August 2012. <http://fivepoetryjournal.tumblr.com/post/28746311293>

– The Ghost in the Library. 5 Poetry Journal, Issue #9. August 2012. <http://fivepoetryjournal.tumblr.com/post/28746311293>

– Post Traumatic Stress. Fortunates, July Issue. July 2012. <http://www.fortunates.org/archives/406>

– Starry Skies. Fortunates, July Issue. July 2012. <http://www.fortunates.org/archives/427>

Alyssa Cooper was born in Belleville Ontario, and has lived in Canada her entire life. A lifelong lover of literature, her first publication came at the age of eighteen, when her poem "Just a Nosebleed" was included in the anthology *Immortal Verses*.

After spending two years studying Fine Arts at York University, she left Toronto to pursue an education in graphic design in Oshawa Ontario. Through the course of her studies, she developed a deep appreciation for book design and bindery, and received formal training in proofreading and editing.

The written word has been her greatest passion since she was a child, when she would carry the novels she could not yet read as part of her wardrobe. She has dedicated her life to developing her voice and pushing the limits of her craft. Her work has been featured in poetry anthologies such as *Journey to Crone* and *Postscripts to Darkness*, and literary magazines such as *The Emrys Journal* and *Revival Literary Journal*. Her first novel, *Salvation*, was released electronically and in print in 2012.

She is currently working as a designer in Belleville, where she lives with her typewriters and personal library.

Books in the North Shore Series
Find full information at
– http://www.HiddenBrookPress.com/b-NShore.html

2 Anthologies

Changing Ways is a book of prose by Cobourg area authors including: Jean Edgar Benitz, Patricia Calder, Fran O'Hara Campbell, Leonard D'Agostino, Shane Joseph, Brian Mullally. Editor: Jacob Hogeterp
  – Prose – ISBN – 978-1-897475-22-5

That Not Forgotten - Editor – Bruce Kauffman with 118 authors from the North Shore geographic area.
  – Prose and Poetry – ISBN – 978-1-897475-89-8

First set of five books

— M.E. Csamer – Kingston – *A Month Without Snow*
  – Prose – ISBN – 978-1-897475-87-2
— Elizabeth Greene – Kingston – *The Iron Shoes*
  – Poetry – ISBN – 978-1-897475-76-6
— Richard Grove – Brighton – *A Family Reunion*
  – Prose – ISBN – 978-1-897475-90-2
— R.D. Roy – Trenton – *A Pre emptive Kindness*
  – Prose – ISBN – 978-1-897475-80-3
— Eric Winter – Cobourg – *The Man In The Hat*
  – Poetry – ISBN – 978-1-897475-77-3

Second set of five books

— Janet Richards – Belleville – *Glass Skin*
  – Poetry – ISBN – 978-1-897475-01-0
— R.D. Roy – Trenton – *Three Cities*
  – Poetry – ISBN – 978-1-897475-96-4
— Wayne Schlepp – Cobourg – *The Darker Edges of the Sky*
  – Poetry – ISBN – 978-1-897475-99-5
— Benjamin Sheedy – Kingston – *A Centre in Which They Breed*
  – Poetry – ISBN – 978-1-897475-98-8
— Patricia Stone – Peterborough – *All Things Considered*
  – Prose – ISBN – 978-1-897475-04-1

Third set of five books

— Mark Clement – Cobourg – *Island In the Shadow*
  – Poetry – ISBN – 978-1-897475-08-9
— Anthony Donnelly – Brighton – *Fishbowl Fridays*
  – Prose – ISBN – 978-1-897475-02-7
— Chris Faiers – Marmora – *ZenRiver Poems & Haibun*
  – Poetry – ISBN – 978-1-897475-25-6
— Shane Joseph – Cobourg – *Fringe Dwellers* Second Edition
  – Prose – ISBN – 978-1-897475-44-7
— Deborah Panko – Cobourg – *Somewhat Elsewhere*
  – Poetry – ISBN – 978-1-897475-13-3

Forth set of five books

— Diane Dawber – Bath – *Driving, Braking and Getting out to Walk*
  – Poetry – ISBN – 978-1-897475-40-9
— Patrick Gray – Port Hope – *This Grace of Light*
  – Poetry – ISBN – 978-1-897475-34-8
— John Pigeau – Kingston – *The Nothing Waltz*
  – Prose – ISBN – 978-1-897475-37-9
— Mike Johnston – Cobourg – *Reflections Around the Sun*
  – Poetry – ISBN – 978-1-897475-38-6
— Kathryn MacDonald – Shannonville – *Calla & Édourd*
  – Prose – ISBN – 978-1-897475-39-3

Fifth set of three books

— Tara Kainer – Kingston – *When I Think On Your Lives*
  – Poetry– ISBN – 978-1-897475-68-3
— Morgan Wade – Kingston – *The Last Stoic*
  – Novel – ISBN – 978-1-897475-63-8
— Kathryn MacDonald – Shannonville – *A Breeze You Whisper*
  – Poetry – ISBN – 978-1-897475-66-9

Sixth set of three books

— Bruce Kauffman – Kingston – *The Texture of Days, in Ash and Leaf*
  – Poetry – ISBN - 978-1-897475-86-7
— Chris Faiers – Marmora – *Eel Pie Island Dharma: A hippie memoir/haibun*
  – A memoir in haibun form – ISBN - 978-1-897475-92-8
— Theodore Michael Christou – Kingston – *an overbearing eye*
  – Poety – ISBN – 978-1-897475-93-5

Seventh set of four books

— Alyssa Cooper – Kingston – *Cold Breath of Life*
  – Poetry – ISBN – 978-1-927725-02-3
— Bruce Kauffman – Kingston – *The Silence Before the Whisper Comes*
  – Poetry – ISBN – 978-1-897475-98-0
— Sarah Richardson – Kingston – *Before I Lose Light*
  – Poetry – ISBN – 978-1-927725-05-4
— G. W. Rasberry – Kingston – *More Naked Than Ever*
  – Poetry – ISBN – 978-1-927725-04-7

www.ingramcontent.com/pod-product-compliance
Lightning Source LLC
Chambersburg PA
CBHW060500080526
44584CB00015B/1499